THE BEST OF

PIANO · VOCAL · GUITAR

ZIGGY MARLEY

AND THE MELODY MAKERS

Photo by Wonder Knack

Cover Photos by Jeffrey Henson Scales

ISBN 0-634-08791-6

HAL•LEONARD®
CORPORATION

7777 W. BLUEMOUND RD. P.O. BOX 13819 MILWAUKEE, WI 53213

In Australia Contact:
Hal Leonard Australia Pty. Ltd.
4 Lentara Court
Cheltenham, Victoria, 3192 Australia
Email: ausadmin@halleonard.com

Visit Hal Leonard Online at
www.halleonard.com

Photo by NUNU

Photo by Wonder Knack

Photo by NUNU

ZIGGY

LUDO

The rules are as follows:
A GAME FOR 2, 3 OR 4 PLAYERS

CONTENTS:
Playboard (included),
1 dice and 16 counters
with 4 sets of colours (not included)

OBJECT:

Players in turn, race each other around the circuit to be the first to get all of their counters to the HOME base. When counters are knocked off they are returned to the starting square.

PLAY:

Each player picks a set of counters and places them in the Starting Squares of the same colour. Take it in turns to throw. You must throw a 6 before you can move a piece onto the track. Every time you throw a 6 you get another throw and you can move any one counter to the number shown on the dice.

If your Counter lands on one of your opponent's they are knocked off and returned. If one of your counters lands on top of your counters this forms a block. Your block cannot be passed by any of the opponent's pieces.

When a counter goes all the way round the board it can enter the HOME column. To land in the HOME triangle you must throw the exact number.

The winner is the first player to get all four counters into the HOME triangle.

BEAUTIFUL MOTHER NATURE

Words and Music by
ZIGGY MARLEY

beau - ti - ful Moth - er Na - ture.

Still is ___ my...

Play 3 times

BLACK MY STORY
(Not History)

Words and Music by ZIGGY MARLEY
and STEPHEN MARLEY

ry.
ry.
ry.
ry.

What we want to see _____ is
Black my sto - ry,
Black my sto - ry,
Not his - to - ry.

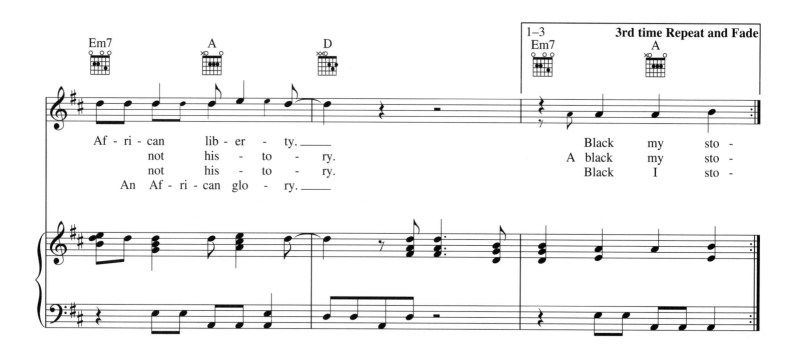

Af - ri - can lib - er - ty. _____
not his - to - ry.
not his - to - ry.
An Af - ri - can glo - ry. _____

1–3   3rd time Repeat and Fade

Black my sto -
A black my sto -
Black I sto -

Optional Ending

Black I sto - ry.   Black my sto - ry!

BROTHERS AND SISTERS

Words and Music by
ZIGGY MARLEY

With a steady beat

I am my ma-ma's son, ___ you are your fa-ther's child. ___ Some - times ___ we act
Some are black and brown, oth - ers white and light. That's all the diff -'rence
I am my fa-ther's son, ___ you are your ma-ma's child. ___ Some - times ___ we act

as if we hate each oth - er. A diff -'rent faith, a diff -'rent state of mind. ___
I can re - mem - ber. A diff -'rent face, a diff -'rent kind of smile. ___
as if we hate each oth - er. A diff -'rent faith, a diff -'rent state of mind. ___

CONSCIOUS PARTY

Words and Music by
ZIGGY MARLEY

JAH BLESS

Words and Music by STEPHEN MARLEY
and VINCENT FORD

Spoken: Let me tell you! Let me tell you something right now!

JOY AND BLUES

Words and Music by ZIGGY MARLEY
and STEPHEN MARLEY

Caribbean Rock beat

KEEP MY FAITH

Words and Music by
ZIGGY MARLEY

Hey!

keep my faith. _   Jah, I keep my faith. _

I'll keep my faith. _

Keep my faith. _   Keep my faith. _

Keep my faith. _   Keep my faith. _

rall.

JUSTICE

Words and Music by
ZIGGY MARLEY

Steady Reggae beat

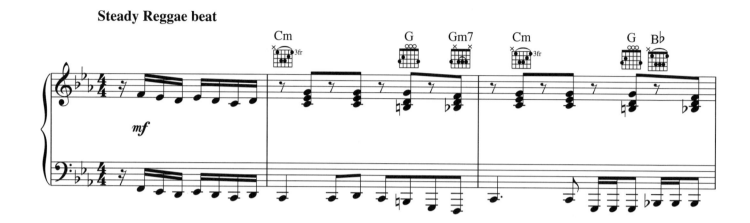

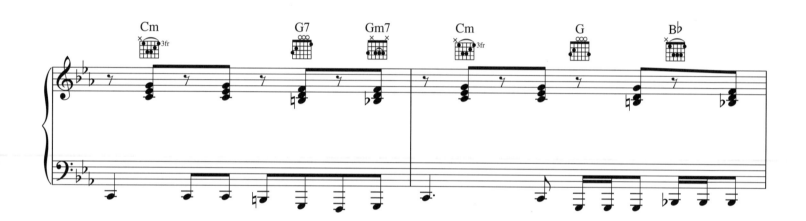

Jus - tice, ___ peo - ple say,
Jus - tice, yeah yeah ___ yeah.

LEE AND MOLLY

Words and Music by
ZIGGY MARLEY

ONE GOOD SPLIFF

Words and Music by
STEPHEN MARLEY

LOOK WHO'S DANCING

Words and Music by ZIGGY MARLEY
and STEPHEN MARLEY

ONE BRIGHT DAY

Words and Music by
ZIGGY MARLEY

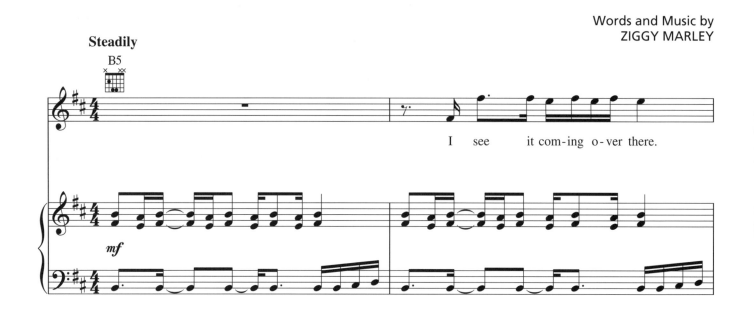

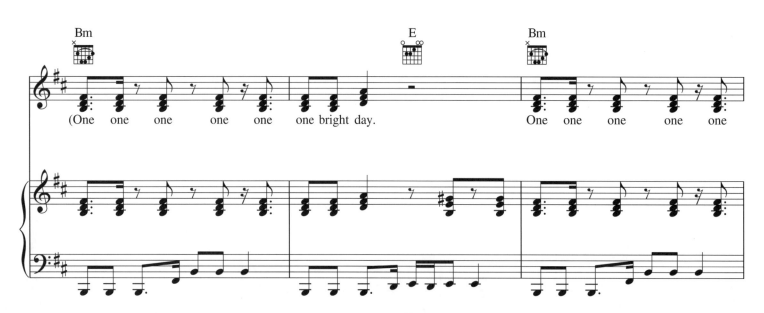

POSTMAN

Words and Music by
STEPHEN MARLEY

Oh, did you get that mes-sage yes-ter-day? _
did you get your mes-sage yes-ter-day? _

Jah sent I as your post - man with your mail. _
Jah sent I as your post - man with your mail. _

Yes he did, _ yeah!
Oh, did you get your mes-sage yes-ter-day? _
Oh, did you get your mes-sage yes-ter-day? _

TIPSY DAZY

Words and Music by
STEPHEN MARLEY

Miss Tip - sy Daz - y, _____
- y, _____
Instrumental solo
- y, _____

you're top - sy - tur - vy. _____
you're top - sy - tur - vy. _____

top - sy - tur - vy, _____

POWER TO MOVE YA

Words and Music by
ZIGGY MARLEY

Rhythmic Afro-Caribbean beat

I got the pow-er to move ___ ya. I got the pow-er to

move ya. ___ I got the pow-er to move ya. ___ Jah got the pow-er to

move ya. ___ Don't take it sim-ple. Bab-y-lon get tram-
So don't you try ___ to stop what you feel ___

SMALL PEOPLE

Words and Music by
ZIGGY MARLEY

(That's how we like it!)

(That's how we like it!)

Small   peo - ple
Walk - ing   down   the   street, _

*Recorded a half step higher.

TOMORROW PEOPLE

Words and Music by
ZIGGY MARLEY

TUMBLIN' DOWN

Words and Music by TYRONE DOWNIE
and ZIGGY MARLEY

here comes the bear, and they're
and their _ big mon - ey. And they
crush the __ op - pres - sor. And I

fight - ing to con - trol the lion's do - min - ion. _____
want to con - trol ou - r bod - y and soul. ____
bet they did - n't know it was mind o - ver mat - ter.

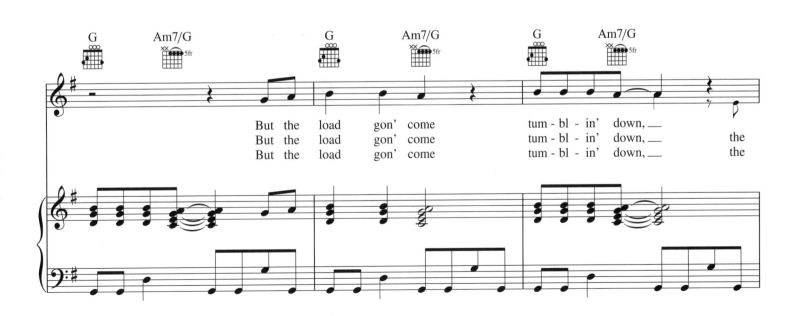

But the load gon' come tum - bl - in' down, ___
But the load gon' come tum - bl - in' down, ___ the
But the load gon' come tum - bl - in' down, ___ the

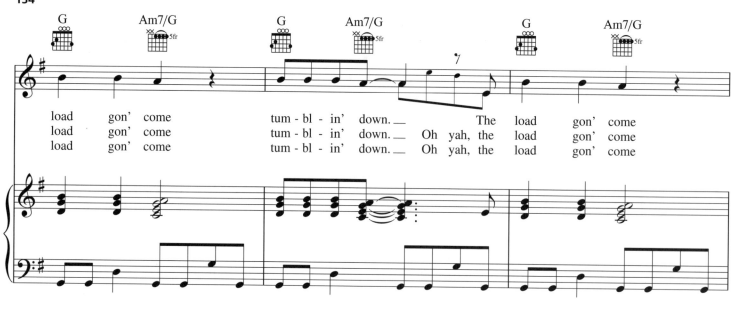

load gon' come
load gon' come
load gon' come

tum - bl - in' down.__ The load gon' come
tum - bl - in' down.__ Oh yah, the load gon' come
tum - bl - in' down.__ Oh yah, the load gon' come

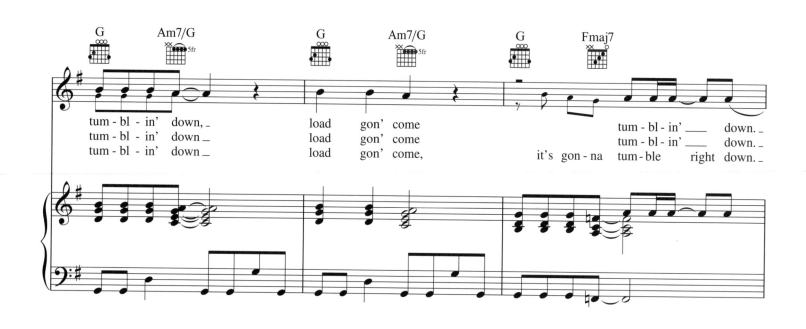

tum - bl - in' down,__ load gon' come
tum - bl - in' down __ load gon' come
tum - bl - in' down __ load gon' come,

tum - bl - in' ___ down. _
tum - bl - in' ___ down. _
it's gon - na tum - ble right down. _

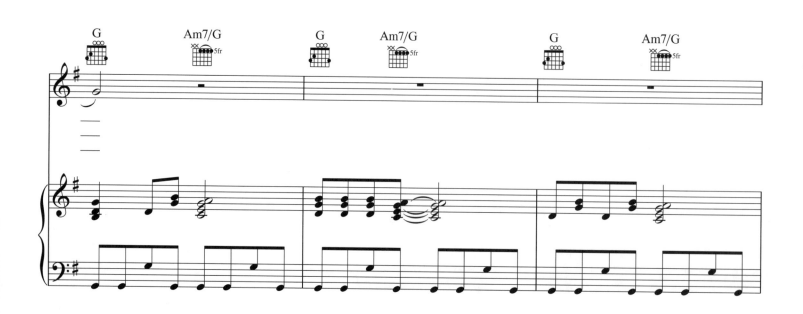